small cakes

small cakes

FROM FONDANT FANCIES TO FLORENTINES

ROGER PIZEY

Photography by Sian Irvine

jacqui small

DEDICATION
For my dad, Eric

First published in 2008 by Jacqui Small LLP
an imprint of Aurum Press
7 Greenland Street
London NW1 0ND

Publisher   Jacqui Small
Commissioning Editor   Joanna Copestick
Editorial Manager   Judith Hannam
Editor   Helen Ridge
Art Director   Ashley Western
Stylist   Roisin Nield
Photography   Sian Irvine
Production   Peter Colley

ISBN: 978 1 90322 1 990

2011 2010 2009 2008

10 9 8 7 6 5 4 3 2 1

Printed in China

Unless otherwise stated, eggs should be
medium (large in the US).

contents

introduction

This book is not meant for just special occasions. It is also for everyday treats, from afternoon tea with friends to baking with children purely for fun.

Baking is an inherent part of every culture, and special recipes are passed down from generation to generation, often playing a part in the rites of passage that children share with their parents or grandparents. For me, much of the joy of baking is using these old recipes to create something delicious to enjoy with family and friends.

I have chosen to include a number of traditional recipes, such as Shortbread, Dundee cake, Eccles cakes and Parkin, because I feel passionately that we should not forget how to bake them. Although these can all now be bought in supermarkets, they are very easy to make at home and are much tastier, healthier and more nutritious than anything mass-produced.

I have also included family favourites such as Cupcakes, Muffins and Brownies, as well as continental treats like Financiers and Madeleines. The cakes and treats are shown baked in a variety of different shapes and sizes. Don't worry if you don't have the tin or mould mentioned in the recipe – just use something of a comparable size.

You will see that I have basically followed two different baking methods: the traditional creaming of butter and sugar, slowly adding the eggs to form a light creamy mixture before folding in the dry ingredients, and the slightly easier and quicker way of combining most of the ingredients before adding the melted butter at the end. Both methods give great results and neither is difficult, but for the grander cakes I think the traditional approach is well worth the time and effort, as it gives a more intense flavour and a better texture.

Above all, I want baking to be a pleasure and a joy, and it is ultimately so rewarding when your friends and family appreciate the effort you have gone to. Enjoy!

ROGER PIZEY

essential equipment

I have used a range of different equipment for making the recipes in this book, and you will probably find that you already have many of the items in your kitchen cupboards. There are certain pieces, though, that I believe are essential for good home baking.

A **muffin tray** is a must – there are so many different muffin recipes around that you are sure to use yours again and again.

The greater the variety of **tart rings** (or, if you prefer, **springform tins**) and **cake tins** in your cupboard, the more fun you'll have with cake shapes and sizes – a varied selection features in this book. It really comes down to personal preference which ones you bake with, but for longevity, it makes sense to invest in those made of good-quality stainless steel.

A recent welcome addition to the domestic kitchen has been non-stick **silicone moulds** and **silicone mats**. These are very easy to use, maintain and store, and are readily available from good kitchen shops. Silicone mats are ideal for baking biscuits and using under tart rings to prevent sticking during baking.

I like to have **hand whisks** of various sizes: a medium one is good for whipping, while a larger balloon whisk is best for folding in ingredients. I always use a **pastry scraper** for scraping down the bowl while incorporating ingredients – my preference is made by Matfer out of polyon, which ensures you get every last bit of the delicious mixture into the oven.

I have a selection of **piping (pastry) bags** and **nozzles (tips)**, and these can be disposable or washable. It's a good idea to have a small, medium and large nozzle (tip) to cover most piping options.

In a few recipes, I have suggested using a **bain-marie (water bath)**. This is simply a method for melting chocolate without it burning. Bring a small pan of water to a simmer. Place your chocolate in a heat-resistant bowl, which should be bigger than the pan, and cover with clingfilm (plastic wrap). Place the bowl on top of the simmering pan of water and the chocolate will melt slowly.

Good knives are always highly recommended in the kitchen. They make cooking in general so much easier, and a large and a small palette knife (flexible metal spatula), with a round end are vital for spreading cream, icing, frosting, etc. When covering a whole cake with something like ganache, a step-down (bent-end) palette knife is good to have.

A **probe thermometer** is a worthwhile and inexpensive purchase that is used not only when making sugar syrup but also for jam and even checking the core temperature of your roast.

Finally, a good **food mixer** makes baking a joy. My personal preference is a Kitchen Aid, although the variety and quality of mixers on the market these days is excellent. Whichever you choose, make sure there is a whisk attachment for creaming and making meringues, and also a paddle attachment for beating.

cupcakes & muffins

ICED CUPCAKES

Everyone loves cupcakes, and I like to make mine look as vivid as possible with toppings in a variety of colours and flavours, from pastel pistachio to sumptuous strawberry, bringing a splash of colour to the tea table.

VANILLA CUPCAKES

Makes 8

2 eggs
175g (generous $^3/_4$ cup) caster (superfine) sugar
140g ($1^1/_4$ cups) plain (all-purpose) flour, sifted
small pinch of table salt
$^1/_2$ tsp baking powder
75ml (5 tbsp) double (heavy) cream
50g ($^1/_4$ cup) unsalted butter, melted
few drops of good-quality vanilla essence

Preheat the oven to 180°C/350°F/ Gas 4. In a mixer, whisk the eggs with the sugar until fully blended. Add the flour, salt and baking powder a little at a time, and whisk together. Mix in the cream, then fold in the melted butter. Finally, add a few drops of vanilla essence.

Place muffin cases in a muffin tray and fill three-quarters full with the mixture. Bake for 20 minutes on the middle shelf until golden brown. To test the cakes are cooked, gently push a skewer or small knife through to the centre of one cake – it should come away clean. Leave the cakes for a minute in the moulds, then turn out onto a wire rack to cool. Decorate with the toppings of your choice (*see right*).

CHOCOLATE CUPCAKES

Makes 6

45g (3 tbsp) unsalted butter, softened
110g (generous $^1/_2$ cup) soft brown sugar
1 egg
20g ($^3/_4$oz) ground almonds
50g ($^1/_2$ cup) self-raising flour, sifted
1 tsp unsweetened cocoa powder
30g (1oz) 70% cocoa dark (bittersweet) chocolate
80ml (5 tbsp + 1 tsp) water

Preheat the oven to 180°C/350°F/ Gas 4. In a mixer, whisk together the softened butter and sugar, then slowly add the egg, followed by the ground almonds, flour and cocoa powder. Melt the chocolate over a bain-marie (water bath) (*see page 8*). Add to the rest of the mixture and blend together.

Place muffin cases in a muffin tray and fill three-quarters full with the mixture. Bake for 20 minutes on the middle shelf. To test the cakes are cooked, gently push a skewer or small knife through to the centre of one cake – it should come away clean. Leave the cakes for a minute in the moulds, then turn out onto a wire rack to cool. Decorate with the toppings of your choice (*see right*).

PEPPERMINT CREAM CHEESE TOPPING

Makes enough for 6 cupcakes

30g (2 tbsp) unsalted butter, softened
80g (3oz) plain cream cheese
250g ($2^1/_4$ cups) icing (confectioners') sugar, sifted
$^1/_2$ tsp peppermint essence
$^1/_2$ tsp green food colouring

Place the softened butter in a mixing bowl. Add the cream cheese and blend together well. Slowly add the icing (confectioners') sugar and peppermint essence. Add the colouring a drop at a time until the mixture reaches the desired green colour. Put the topping in the fridge for about an hour prior to icing (frosting) the cakes.

LEMON BUTTER CREAM TOPPING

Makes enough for 6 cupcakes

30g (2 tbsp) unsalted butter, softened
80g (3oz) plain cream cheese
250g (2$\frac{1}{4}$ cups) icing (confectioners') sugar, sifted
2–3 drops lemon essence
$\frac{1}{2}$ tsp yellow food colouring

Follow the method for the Peppermint Cream Cheese Topping (*see left*).

CLASSIC BUTTER CREAM

Makes enough for 6 cupcakes

60ml (4 tbsp) water
100g ($\frac{1}{2}$ cup) caster (superfine) sugar
230g (1 cup) butter
3 egg yolks

Mix the water and sugar in a pan and bring to the boil. While the sugar is boiling, cut the butter up into cubes and put to one side, then crack the egg yolks into a mixer.

Using a probe thermometer (*see page 8*), check the temperature of the sugar. When it reaches 120ºC/250ºF, whisk the egg yolks on a low speed. Remove the sugar from the heat and slowly start pouring the sugar into the bowl – try to pour it in between the whisk and the bowl. When all the sugar is in, continue to whisk on a high speed until the bowl starts to cool down. Then slowly add the cubed butter until thoroughly mixed in. Stop the machine to scrape down the sides and then mix for a little longer.

Split the butter cream into two bowls, ready for making the blueberry and strawberry toppings (*see right*).

BLUEBERRY TOPPING

Makes enough for 6 cupcakes

200g (7oz) fresh or frozen blueberries
75g (6 tbsp) caster (superfine) sugar
1 tbsp water

Place all the ingredients in a pan and bring slowly to the boil. Simmer for 5 minutes, then place in a blender and blitz with the pulse button. Pass the liquid through a sieve. Return to the pan and gently simmer until the liquid is reduced by about half.

Slowly add the purée to one half of the butter cream (*see left*) with a hand whisk until you're happy with the taste and colour. Place in the fridge for about 30 minutes to cool. Using a large star nozzle (tip), pipe a huge whip onto the top of each cupcake.

STRAWBERRY TOPPING

Makes enough for 6 cupcakes

200g (7oz) fresh or frozen strawberries
75g (6 tbsp) caster (superfine) sugar
1 tbsp water

Follow the method for the Blueberry Topping (*see above*).

RASPBERRY & COCONUT BUNS

Deliciously light and moist, and crammed with a wonderful flavour.

Preheat the oven to 180ºC/350ºF/Gas 4. Cream the butter and sugar together in a mixing bowl until light and fluffy. Add the eggs, followed by both lots of flour and the desiccated coconut. Mix in the sour cream and gently fold in the raspberries, leaving 12 aside for decoration.

Place 6 muffin cases in a muffin tray and fill each case three-quarters full with the mixture. Bake on the middle shelf for approximately 40 minutes. To test the buns are cooked, gently push a skewer or small knife through to the centre of one bun – it should come away clean. Leave the buns for a minute in the moulds, then turn out onto a wire rack to cool.

Using a spatula, spread the cream cheese topping over each bun, sprinkle with some flaked coconut, then pop two raspberries on top for decoration.

Makes 6

125g (generous $\frac{1}{2}$ cup) unsalted butter
220g (generous 1 cup) caster (superfine) sugar
3 eggs, lightly beaten
75g ($\frac{2}{3}$ cup) plain (all-purpose) flour, sifted
40g ($\frac{1}{3}$ cup) self-raising flour, sifted
45g ($1\frac{1}{2}$oz) desiccated coconut
75ml (5 tbsp) sour cream
150g ($5\frac{1}{2}$oz) fresh raspberries
cream cheese topping (follow the recipe for the Peppermint Cream Cheese Topping on page 12 but leave out the peppermint essence and colouring)
a little flaked (slivered) coconut, for decoration

FONDANT FANCIES

Perfect for topping off with the prettiest fondant finishes.

Preheat the oven to 180ºC/350ºF/Gas 4. Mix the egg yolks, milk and vanilla essence together in a bowl. Slowly add the flour, sugar, baking powder and salt. Beat everything together, then add the melted butter and mix in thoroughly.

Place 12 muffin cases in a muffin tray and fill each case three-quarters full with the mixture. Bake for 20 minutes on the middle shelf until golden brown. To test the cakes are cooked, gently push a skewer or small knife through to the centre of one cake – it should come away clean. Leave the cakes for a minute in the moulds, then turn out onto a wire rack to cool.

Place the fondant in a saucepan and add a little water. You can also add a little food colouring for different effects. Warm the fondant through until soft, pliable and shiny, then mould it in the desired design onto the cupcakes.

Makes 12

3 egg yolks
245ml (1 cup + 1 tsp) whole milk
drop of vanilla essence
300g ($2\frac{1}{2}$ cups) plain (all-purpose) flour, sifted
300g ($1\frac{1}{2}$ cups) caster (superfine) sugar
2 tsp baking powder
small pinch of table salt
170g ($\frac{3}{4}$ cup) unsalted butter, melted
500g (1lb 2oz) pack fondant (available from most supermarkets)
few drops of food colouring (optional)

Opposite: Raspberry & Coconut Buns; Fondant Fancies illustrated on page 2

BLUEBERRY MUFFINS

Always a favourite with children and easy to make all year round.

Preheat the oven to 180°C/350°F/Gas 4. Melt the butter in a pan. Remove from the heat and pour into a bowl. Add the eggs, buttermilk and both zests, then the flour, baking powder, sugar and salt, and mix together lightly – do not overmix, as this will make the muffins heavy. Fold in the blueberries (if frozen, roll them in a little flour first to prevent them 'bleeding' through the muffins).

Place 12 muffin cases in a muffin tray and fill each case three-quarters full with the mixture. Bake on the middle shelf for 20–25 minutes. To test the muffins are cooked, gently push a skewer or small knife through to the centre of one muffin – it should come away clean. Leave the muffins for a minute in the moulds, then turn out onto a wire rack to cool.

Makes 12

75g (6 tbsp) unsalted butter
3 eggs, lightly beaten
225ml (scant 1 cup) buttermilk
grated zest 1 lemon
grated zest 1 orange
450g (4 cups) plain (all-purpose) flour, sifted
1 tsp baking powder
75g (6 tbsp) caster (superfine) sugar
1 tsp table salt
225g (8oz) fresh or frozen blueberries

CHOCOLATE MUFFINS

Laced with chocolate chips, how could anyone refuse…?

Preheat the oven to 180°C/350°F/Gas 4. Melt the butter in a pan. Remove from the heat and pour into a bowl. Add the eggs and milk, followed by the flour, baking powder, sugar and cocoa powder, and mix together lightly – do not overmix, as this will make the muffins heavy. Fold in the chocolate chips.

Place 12 muffin cases in a muffin tray and fill each case three-quarters full with the mixture. Bake on the middle shelf for 20–25 minutes. To test the muffins are cooked, gently push a skewer or small knife through to the centre of one muffin – it should come away clean. Leave the muffins for a minute in the moulds, then turn out onto a wire rack to cool.

Makes 12

80g (6 tbsp) unsalted butter
2 eggs, lightly beaten
300ml (1 cup + 4 tbsp) whole milk
300g (2^1/$_2$ cups) plain (all-purpose) flour, sifted
2 tsp baking powder
150g (^{3}/$_4$ cup) caster (superfine) sugar
40g (1^1/$_4$ oz) cup) unsweetened cocoa powder
120g (4^1/$_2$ oz) dark chocolate chips
100g (3^1/$_2$ oz) white chocolate chips

cakes for sharing

CHOCOLATE LAYER CAKE

Melt-in-the-mouth indulgence – this is probably the richest cake in the book. Using hazelnut powder instead of flour gives a very rich sponge, which should be cut into thin slices when serving.

Preheat the oven to 170°C/340°F/Gas 3. Bring the water to the boil in a pan, add the cocoa powder and stir to form a paste. Stir in the vanilla seeds. Remove from the heat and leave to cool.

Meanwhile, in a mixing bowl, soften the butter with a spatula, then add about one-third of the sugar. Cream together. Add the egg yolks, beat the mixture, then fold in the hazelnut powder. Add the cooled cocoa powder paste.

In a mixer, whisk the egg whites, adding the rest of the sugar slowly once the whites start to peak, followed by the cream of tartar. (The cream of tartar acts as a stabilizer and strengthens the egg whites.) Whisk until stiff. Fold the egg whites into the yolk mixture. Line the bottom of a loaf tin, measuring 25 x 8 x 8cm deep (10 x 3 x 3in), with parchment paper and pour in the mixture. Bake on the middle shelf for approximately 45 minutes. Leave to cool in the tin for 10 minutes, then turn out onto a wire rack and strip off the parchment paper. When cold, square off the sides of the sponge with a knife and cut in half lengthways.

Meanwhile, toast the hazelnut flakes for the decoration and make the ganache (*see right*).

Place one sponge on a cake board and use a palette knife (flexible metal spatula) to spread one-third of the ganache over the top. Place the second sponge on top of the first and spread a second layer of ganache over the top. With the remaining ganache, completely cover the sides of the cake and smooth all the surfaces. Sprinkle the toasted hazelnut flakes over the top, pressing down gently to ensure they stick.

Serves 8

50ml (3 tbsp + 1 tsp) water
25g (1oz) unsweetened cocoa powder
1/2 vanilla pod, split and scraped
115g (1/2 cup) unsalted butter
115g (generous 1/2 cup) caster (superfine) sugar
3 eggs, separated
85g (3oz) hazelnut powder, toasted and cooled (if unavailable, use whole hazelnuts and roast in the oven, leave to cool and blitz in a blender with the pulse button)
1/2 tsp cream of tartar

For the decoration
75g (2 1/2 oz) hazelnut flakes

Spread the hazelnut flakes on a baking tray. Bake on the top shelf for approximately 10 minutes until golden brown. Leave to cool.

For the ganache
110g (4oz) 70% cocoa dark (bittersweet) chocolate
125ml (1/2 cup) double (heavy) cream
40g (3 tbsp) unsalted butter

Melt the chocolate slowly over a bain-marie (water bath). In a separate pan, bring the cream to the boil, then pour over the melted chocolate and start to stir. Slowly add the butter and bring together until the chocolate starts to thicken. Remove from the heat.

ROULE MARQUISE

A wonderfully pleasurable summer treat that always elicits the wickedest smile when first served, and it never disappoints!

Preheat the oven to 170°C/340°F/Gas 3. In a large mixing bowl, whisk the egg yolks together with one-third of the icing (confectioners') sugar to create a thick sabayon. In a separate bowl, whisk the egg whites until they form soft peaks, then add the rest of the icing (confectioners') sugar. Fold the egg white mixture into the sabayon, then slowly fold in the sifted cocoa powder and cornflour (cornstarch).

Cut parchment paper to the size of your baking tray (this recipe fits a tray approximately 40 x 30cm/16 x 12in). Blob a little of the mixture onto each corner of the baking tray, then place the paper on top (this prevents the paper from moving in the oven). Pour the mixture onto the paper and, using a palette knife (flexible metal spatula), spread the mixture evenly. Bake on the middle shelf for 20 minutes. Meanwhile, make the sugar syrup and chantilly cream (*see right*).

Remove the sponge from the oven. If it is ready, the sponge will spring back when pressed lightly. Turn out immediately, parchment paper-side up, onto a clean tea towel. Make a slit in the centre of the paper with a knife. Starting from the slit, carefully peel the parchment paper away from the sponge.

While the sponge is still warm, dip a pastry brush into the sugar syrup and dab the sponge until moist but not soaked. Next, brush on a layer of warmed raspberry jam and, finally, spread a layer of chantilly cream using a palette knife (flexible metal spatula). Stud with fresh raspberries.

Pick up the far edges of the tea towel and slowly bring it towards you to curl the sponge into a roll. Wrap the tea towel around the roll and place in the fridge to set and absorb all the flavours.

Serves 8

4 eggs, separated
250g (2$^1/_4$ cups) icing (confectioners') sugar
100g (3$^1/_2$ oz) unsweetened cocoa powder, sifted
25g ($^1/_4$ cup) cornflour (cornstarch), sifted
150g (5$^1/_2$ oz) seedless raspberry jam, warmed
fresh raspberries, for decoration (optional)

For the sugar syrup
100g (generous $^1/_2$ cup) caster (superfine) sugar
100ml (6 tbsp + 2 tsp) water

Place the sugar and water in a pan. Cook over a low heat until clear, stirring continuously, then boil for a minute or so. Pass the liquid through a sieve. Remove from the heat and leave to cool.

For the chantilly cream
500ml (2 cups) double (heavy) cream
65g (9 tbsp) icing (confectioners') sugar, sifted
1 tsp good-quality vanilla essence

Whisk the cream in a mixing bowl. Slowly add the icing (confectioners') sugar and vanilla essence, and whisk until the mixture becomes quite stiff.

STRAWBERRY SANDWICH CAKE

An elegant teatime extravagance that hits the eye first and the mouth second. It's ideally served on those especially beautiful summer days.

Preheat the oven to 170ºC/340ºF/Gas 3. In a mixing bowl, whisk the eggs and icing (confectioners') sugar together until light, fluffy and quite stiff. Slowly fold in the flour, followed by the melted butter. Place a lightly greased 16 x 3.5cm deep (6^1/$_2$ x 1^1/$_2$in) tart ring (see page 8) on a lightly greased baking tray and pour in the mixture. Bake on the middle shelf for 20 minutes or until golden and springy to the touch. Leave to cool in the ring for about 10 minutes, then turn out carefully onto a wire rack.

Cut off the tops of the strawberries and slice thinly lengthways. Slice off the raised part of the sponge to make it level, then slice the sponge horizontally through the middle. Place one half white-side up back into the tart ring. Dip a pastry brush into the sugar syrup and dab the sponge until moist but not soaked. Next, brush on a layer of strawberry jam. Arrange the strawberries, side-by-side, flat sides facing out, all around the edge of the sponge.

Using a small palette knife (flexible metal spatula), smooth half the chantilly cream over the base of the sponge and arrange the rest of the strawberries, flat sides down, over the top. Spoon the rest of the cream onto the centre of the sponge and spread it over evenly, pushing some of it through the gaps between the strawberries to give a flush finish. Smooth over the top of the cream. Place the second half of the sponge brown-side up over the cream. Press down lightly on the top to ensure a nice flat surface. Place in the fridge until ready to serve.

To serve, remove the ring, sprinkle the top with icing (confectioners') sugar and garnish with a nice big strawberry, dipped in either a raspberry coulis or neutral glaze.

Serves 8

2 eggs
65g (9 tbsp) icing (confectioners') sugar, sifted, + extra for dusting
65g (9 tbsp) plain (all-purpose) flour, sifted
10g (1 tbsp) unsalted butter, melted
sugar syrup (see page 23), made with 100g (generous ^{1}/$_2$ cup) caster (superfine) sugar and 100ml (6 tbsp + 2 tsp) water
chantilly cream (see page 23), made using half the ingredients
270g (9^1/$_4$oz) strawberries
50g (1^3/$_4$oz) seedless strawberry jam, warmed
1 large strawberry, for decoration
raspberry coulis (see below) or a neutral glaze (available from good supermarkets)

For the raspberry coulis
200g (1 cup) caster (superfine) sugar
500g (1lb 2oz) fresh or frozen raspberries

Place the sugar and raspberries in a blender. Blitz with the pulse button, then pass through a sieve.

MERINGUES WITH PASSION FRUIT COULIS

Blow away any memories of traditional meringues and feast on these spectacular delights, which will not only dazzle the eye but blast the taste buds, too. As well as tasting divine, they're very easy to make.

Preheat the oven to 100°C/212°F/Gas ¼. Place the egg whites in a mixer and whisk. After they froth and begin to fold in on themselves, slowly add the sugar. Whisk until stiff peaks form, then slowly whisk in the lemon juice. Scoop out a large serving spoon of the mixture for each meringue and drop onto a non-stick baking tray or silicone mat (*see page 8*). Create peaks by gently touching the mixture with the back of the spoon and lifting it away.

Bake on the middle shelf for about 2 hours. If you like your meringues a little chewy, remove them at this point and leave to cool on a wire rack. If you prefer them crunchier, leave in the oven a little longer.

Meanwhile, make the coulis. When ready to serve, dribble a tablespoon of the coulis over the top of each meringue.

Makes 6

10 egg whites
550g (4¾ cups) icing (confectioners') sugar
2 tsp lemon juice

For the coulis
7 passion fruit
caster (superfine) sugar, to taste
1 tbsp orange juice

Cut the passion fruit in half and scrape out the seeds and pink flesh. Using a blender, blitz the fruit with the pulse button until the flesh comes away from the seeds but the seeds remain whole. Pass through a sieve, ensuring you keep all the delicious juice. Add sugar to the juice in a ratio of approximately 2:1 juice to sugar, according to taste. Pour into a pan with the orange juice and bring to the boil, whisking continuously until the quantity is reduced by half. Remove from the heat and leave to cool.

PROFITEROLES WITH CHANTILLY CREAM & CHOCOLATE SAUCE

This classic recipe from the 1970s tastes as good now as it did then, and I believe it's in need of a revival. So get baking and wow your friends!

To make the choux pastry, place the water, butter, sugar and salt in a pan and bring to the boil, making sure the butter is melted. Add the flour and stir in with a wooden spoon – it is important to cook the flour fully, so don't hurry this process. The dough should come away easily from the side of the pan.

Place the dough in a mixer and, while beating, slowly add enough egg to make it suitable for piping – if it's too wet, you won't be able to pipe it. Cover with clingfilm (plastic wrap) and leave to rest in the fridge. Fit a piping (pastry) bag with a large nozzle (tip), and half-fill the bag with the cooled mixture.

Holding the bag almost vertically and about 1cm ($^1/_2$in) above a baking tray, pipe a bulb of choux approximately 2.5cm (1in) wide and 2cm ($^3/_4$in) high. Space more bulbs evenly on the tray. (If you have a non-stick baking tray, you can pipe straight onto the tray. If not, cut a piece of parchment paper the size of the tray and fix it on using a few blobs of the choux dough – this will make it easier to pipe and stop the paper blowing in the oven.) Preheat the oven to 250°C/480°F/Gas 9.

Using a pastry brush, apply a little whisked egg as a wash over the bulbs, dabbing the tops and flattening down any spikes to create a smoother surface when cooked. Place on the middle shelf of the oven and turn off the oven. Leave for 15–20 minutes and then turn the oven back on at 180°C/350°F/Gas 4 – this makes the choux rise slowly and uniformly. Bake for at least another 20 minutes. Do not open the door until nearly cooked or the choux will flatten. Taste one of the choux – it should be crunchy and cooked in the middle. Remove from the oven and turn out onto a wire rack. Meanwhile, make the chantilly cream (*see page 23*) and the chocolate sauce (*see right*).

When the choux buns are completely cooled, use a pair of scissors to push a hole into the bottom of each one. Pipe the chantilly cream into each of the buns, making sure they are full. Pile in a mound and pour over the warm chocolate sauce.

Makes approximately 15

150ml ($^2/_3$ cup) water
60g ($^1/_3$ cup) unsalted butter
2 tsp caster (superfine) sugar
good pinch of table salt
100g ($^3/_4$ cup) strong white (bread) flour
2–3 eggs, whisked
chantilly cream (*see page 23*), made using half the ingredients

For the chocolate sauce
200g (7oz) 70% cocoa dark (bittersweet) chocolate
120ml ($^1/_2$ cup) whole milk
30ml (2 tbsp) double (heavy) cream
30g (2 tbsp) caster (superfine) sugar
30g (2 tbsp) unsalted butter

Melt the chocolate over a bain-marie (water bath) (*see page 8*). In a separate pan, heat the milk, cream and sugar. Pour the mixture onto the melted chocolate and mix together using a whisk. Slowly whisk in the butter.

VANILLA CHEESECAKE

The American classic. Smooth, rich and easy to make, it can be a special treat for dessert or a delicious delight in the afternoon. Served with a blueberry compote, this is the perfect cheesecake every time.

Preheat the oven to 140°C/275°F/Gas 1. Melt the butter in a pan. Pour over the crushed digestive biscuits (graham crackers) and mix together. Place a 16 x 3.5cm deep (6$^{1}/_{2}$ x 1$^{1}/_{2}$in) lightly greased tart ring (*see page 8*) on a lightly greased baking tray. Spread the biscuit mixture evenly in the ring.

In a mixing bowl, soften the cream cheese with a spatula. In a separate bowl, mix the vanilla seeds with the sugar, then add to the bowl of cream cheese. Add the sour cream and egg, and beat slowly for a short time – do not overbeat, as too much air will result in a soufflé. Fill the ring with the mixture and smooth over using a palette knife (flexible metal spatula). Bake on the middle shelf for 40 minutes.

To check that the cheesecake is cooked, gently push a small knife into the centre – it should come away clean. Leave the cheesecake to cool for 20 minutes before placing in the fridge. Remove the ring just before serving. Serve with a blueberry compote (*see right*).

Serves 6

40g (3 tbsp) unsalted butter
100g (3$^{1}/_{2}$ oz) digestive biscuits (graham crackers), crushed
600g (1lb 5oz) plain cream cheese
$^{1}/_{2}$ vanilla pod, split and scraped
80g (6 tbsp) caster (superfine) sugar
80ml (5 tbsp) sour cream
1 egg

For the blueberry compote
500g (1lb 2oz) fresh or frozen blueberries
75g (6 tbsp) caster (superfine) sugar
1 tbsp water

Place 200g (7oz) of blueberries and the sugar and water in a pan and bring slowly to the boil. Simmer for 5 minutes, then leave to cool for 10 minutes. Blitz in a blender with the pulse button, then pass through a sieve. Return to the pan and gently simmer until the quantity is reduced by about half. Add the remaining blueberries and bring to the boil. Remove from the heat and allow to cool.

CHOCOLATE CHEESECAKE

For me, this recipe is a wonderful alternative to baked cheesecake. The Grand Marnier and chocolate are perfectly matched and, with the extra surprise of the crunchy praline bottom, it's sure to be a favourite.

Pour the melted white chocolate over the crushed cornflakes. Add the praline paste and mix thoroughly.

Place a 26 x 3.5cm deep (10 x 1^1/$_2$in) tart ring (*see page 8*) on a slightly larger cake board. Spoon the cornflake mixture into the ring and, with the back of the spoon, smooth it evenly across the bottom of the ring. If the mixture sticks to the spoon, dip the spoon in warm water.

Soften the gelatin leaves in a bowl of very cold water (if using powdered gelatin, mix it into a paste with a little cold water). Meanwhile, in a mixing bowl, soften the cream cheese with a spatula, then add the sifted sugar. In a pan, warm the Grand Marnier, add the softened gelatin leaves (or the gelatin paste) and dissolve thoroughly. Remove from the heat and whisk gently into the cream cheese mixture. Add the melted chocolate and fold in the whipped cream. Pour the mixture into the ring and smooth over with a palette knife (flexible metal spatula). Leave to set in the fridge for 3 hours. Just before serving, remove the ring. If you wish, add a little decoration, such as orange confit or candied orange peel.

Serves 10

30g (1oz) white chocolate, melted
75g (2^1/$_2$oz) cornflakes, crushed
50g (1^3/$_4$oz) praline paste (available from large supermarkets)
1^1/$_2$ bronze gelatin leaves (available from large supermarkets) or 2 tsp powdered gelatin
350g (12^1/$_2$oz) plain cream cheese
100g (generous ^{3}/$_4$ cup) icing (confectioners') sugar, sifted
70ml (5 tbsp) Grand Marnier liqueur
100g (3^1/$_2$oz) 70% cocoa dark (bittersweet) chocolate, melted
280ml (1 cup + 2 tbsp) double (heavy) cream, whipped to a 'ribbon'
orange confit or candied orange peel (optional)

BAKEWELL TART

A classic tart that's equally good when it's dressed down for afternoon tea or up for dinner. I like to serve it hot or cold with crème anglaise.

Make the sweet pastry 24 hours ahead of time. I also like to make my Bakewell mix the day before to give it time to rest and prevent a soufflé effect during baking, but a few hours ahead should be enough.

For the sweet pastry, cream the butter and sugar together. Add the egg yolks and half the water. Mix in the flour slowly, then the rest of the water. Knead slowly on a floured work surface. Wrap in clingfilm (plastic wrap) and refrigerate for 24 hours.

For the Bakewell mix, cream the butter and sugar together in a mixer until light and fluffy, then add the ground almonds and sifted flours. Whisk together well, then slowly whisk in the eggs until fully blended. Place in the fridge to rest.

On a lightly floured surface, roll out the sweet pastry to about 3mm ($^1/_8$in) thick. Dust it with flour as you roll to prevent it from sticking. Place a 26 x 1cm deep (10 x $^1/_2$in) tart ring (*see page 8*) on top of the pastry and cut a circle out of the pastry 2cm ($^3/_4$in) wider all round than the ring. Line a baking tray with parchment paper and place the ring on top. Place the pastry over the top of the ring. With thumbs and forefingers, gently push the pastry down all around to the edges of the ring. Refrigerate for 2 hours.

Preheat the oven to 170°C/340°F/Gas 3. Remove the pastry from the fridge. Line the base and sides with parchment paper, then fill with baking beans (dried haricot beans, lentils or rice work just as well). Bake-blind for approximately 25 minutes until lightly brown on the bottom. Remove from the oven and leave to cool. Remove the beans and parchment paper.

Lower the oven temperature to 160°C/325°F/Gas 2$^1/_2$. Spread the raspberry jam over the sweet pastry, then cover with the Bakewell mix. Bake on the middle shelf for 10 minutes. Remove and sprinkle liberally with flaked (slivered) almonds (if the almonds are on the tart for the full cooking time, they will burn). Return to the oven for a further 30 minutes or until the tart is firm to the touch. Remove and leave to cool for 20 minutes before turning out onto a wire rack. Strip off the parchment paper.

Serves 8

For the sweet pastry
220g (1 cup) unsalted butter
90g ($^3/_4$ cup) icing (confectioners') sugar
2 egg yolks
25ml (5 tsp) water
300g (2$^1/_2$ cups) plain (all-purpose) flour, sifted

For the Bakewell mix
250g (generous 1 cup) unsalted butter
250g (1$^1/_4$ cups) caster (superfine) sugar
120g (4$^1/_2$oz) ground almonds
60g (9 tbsp) rice flour, sifted
60g (9 tbsp) self-raising flour, sifted
3 eggs
540g (1lb 3oz) seedless raspberry jam, warmed
180g (6$^1/_2$oz) flaked (slivered) almonds

For the crème anglaise
65g (5 tbsp) caster (superfine) sugar
3 egg yolks
240ml (1 cup) whole milk
1 vanilla pod, split and scraped

In a bowl, whisk together the sugar and egg yolks until light in colour. In a pan, bring the milk to the boil with the vanilla seeds. Pour onto the mixture, return to the pan and warm on a low heat. Stir continuously until the mixture coats the back of the spoon. Remove from the heat and sieve.

cakes for slicing

PISTACHIO & LEMON CAKE

A delightfully tangy teatime treat with a fantastic combination of flavours.

Preheat the oven to 160°C/325°F/Gas 2$^{1}/_{2}$. Place the lemon and lime slices and sugar syrup in a saucepan and gently simmer for 10 minutes. Drain and leave to cool.

In a bowl, cream the butter and sugar together until light and fluffy, then add the eggs slowly. Sift in the flour, salt and baking powder, then add two-thirds of the chopped pistachios, the zests and lemon juice. (I like to use the more expensive pistachios for this recipe, as their emerald green colour is so inviting.) Mix well.

Line a 16 x 6cm deep (6$^{1}/_{2}$ x 2$^{1}/_{4}$in) cake tin with parchment paper. Pour in the mixture, place the fruit slices on the top and sprinkle with the remaining pistachios.

Bake on the middle shelf for 40 minutes. To test the cake is cooked, gently push a knife through to the centre – it should come away clean. Leave to cool in the tin for 15 minutes, then turn out onto a wire rack and strip off the parchment paper.

Serves 8

1 lemon, sliced
1 lime, sliced
sugar syrup (*see page 23*), made with 100g (generous $^{1}/_{2}$ cup) caster (superfine) sugar and 100ml (6 tbsp + 2 tsp) water
125g ($^{2}/_{3}$ cup) unsalted butter
175g (generous $^{3}/_{4}$ cup) caster (superfine) sugar
3 eggs, lightly beaten
125g (generous 1 cup) plain (all-purpose) flour
pinch of table salt
$^{1}/_{2}$ tsp baking powder
125g (4$^{1}/_{2}$oz) good-quality pistachios, chopped
juice and grated zest of 1 lemon
grated zest of 1 lime

PLUM MADEIRA

Also delicious as a dessert served with crème fraîche or custard.

Preheat the oven to 160°C/325°F/Gas 2$^{1}/_{2}$. Cut the plums into quarters, removing the stones. Cream the butter and sugar together until light and fluffy, and add the eggs slowly, one at a time. (Ideally, the eggs should be at room temperature so as not to curdle the mixture. If it does curdle, just add a little flour and beat to bring it back together.) Sift the flour and baking powder together, add the oatmeal, Madeira, orange zest and juice, and fold into the mixture.

Line a 16 x 6cm deep (6$^{1}/_{2}$ x 2$^{1}/_{4}$in) cake tin with parchment paper. Pour in the mixture and stud with the plum quarters along the top. Bake on the middle shelf for about 40 minutes. To test the cake is cooked, gently push a knife through to the centre – it should come away clean. Leave to cool in the tin for 15 minutes, then turn out onto a wire rack and strip off the parchment paper.

Serves 8

200g (7oz) plums
100g (scant $^{1}/_{2}$ cup) unsalted butter
100g (generous $^{3}/_{4}$ cup) icing (confectioners') sugar
2 eggs
125g (generous 1 cup) self-raising flour
$^{1}/_{2}$ tsp baking powder
50g (1$^{3}/_{4}$oz) oatmeal
$^{1}/_{2}$ tbsp Madeira
grated zest of 1 orange + 4 tbsp juice

Opposite: Plum Madeira; Pistachio & Lemon Cake illustrated on pages 36–7

RHUBARB CRUMBLE CAKE

I love rhubarb, and I wanted to create a recipe that included its unique flavour. Using crumble on the top blends the traditional with the new, giving a delicious combination of crunch, crumble and tartness.

Preheat the oven to 170°C/340°F/Gas 3. Wash and cut the rhubarb into 2.5cm (1in) strips. (If the rhubarb is very green, peel before chopping.) Place on a baking tray and sprinkle with 140g (scant $^3/_4$ cup) of the caster (superfine) sugar and orange juice. Cover with aluminium foil and bake for 20 minutes. Remove from the oven and drain the juices.

Meanwhile, cream the butter and remaining caster sugar together in a mixing bowl until light and fluffy, then gradually add the eggs. Fold in the flour, lemon zest and ground almonds, followed by the milk. Mix together. Place the mixture into a lightly greased 16 x 6cm deep ($6^1/_2$ x $2^1/_4$in) cake tin.

To make the crumble topping, mix together the ground almonds, sugar and flour, then slowly rub in the butter using your fingertips until the mixture resembles breadcrumbs.

Spread the cooked rhubarb evenly over the cake mixture, followed by an even layer of the crumble topping. Bake on the middle shelf for 40 minutes.

Serves 8

220g (8oz) rhubarb
265g (generous $1^1/_4$ cups) caster (superfine) sugar
5 tsp orange juice
175g ($^3/_4$ cup) unsalted butter
3 eggs, lightly beaten
175g ($1^1/_2$ cups) self-raising flour, sifted
grated zest of 1 lemon
60g (2oz) ground almonds
60ml (4 tbsp) whole milk

For the crumble topping
60g (2oz) ground almonds
50g ($^1/_4$ cup) caster (superfine) sugar
80g ($^2/_3$ cup) plain (all-purpose) flour
50g ($^1/_4$ cup) unsalted butter, diced

DUNDEE CAKE

Bursting with fruit, moist and lightly spiced, this is spongier than a traditional fruit cake but has a great flavour and crumbly texture.

Preheat the oven to 160°C/325°F/Gas 2½. Using a mixer, cream the butter and sugar together until light and fluffy. Beat in the eggs slowly, one at a time. Sift the flour and baking powder together and add to the mixture. Add in all the fruit, ground almonds, zest and sherry. Mix together well. Put to one side.

Spread the blanched almonds on an oven tray and toast them on the top shelf in the oven for 15 minutes or until golden brown.

This recipe works perfectly with a 14 x 6.5cm deep (5½ x 2½in) hexagonal cake tin (*see page 8*). Alternatively, use a 16 x 6.5cm deep (6½ x 2½in) round cake tin. Line the tin with parchment paper, making sure there are not too many creases in the corners – cut the paper down with a knife. Fill with the mixture and stud the toasted almonds in two concentric circles on the top of the cake. Bake for at least 1 hour on the middle shelf.

Test the cake is cooked by inserting a knife into the centre – it should come away clean. Place on a wire rack and, after a few minutes, remove from the tin and strip off the parchment paper. Brush the top with the warmed apricot jam.

Serves 8

150g (10 tbsp) unsalted butter
150g (¾ cup) caster (superfine) sugar
3 eggs
225g (2 cups) plain (all-purpose) flour
1 tsp baking powder
175g (6oz) currants
175g (6oz) sultanas (golden raisins)
50g (1¾ oz) glacé (candied) cherries, quartered
2 tbsp ground almonds
grated zest 1 lemon
grated zest 1 orange
2 tbsp dry sherry or similar spirit (optional)

For the decoration
30–40 whole blanched almonds
3 tbsp apricot jam, sieved and warmed

RICH FRUIT CAKE

It's a good idea to make this cake well in advance, as its flavour matures and improves over time. If you want to make a larger, celebration cake, all you have to do is increase the quantities proportionately.

Preheat the oven to 160°C/325°F/Gas 2½. Place the whole almonds on a baking tray and toast them on the top shelf until golden brown. In a bowl, mix all the fruit together with the flour, baking powder, salt, mixed spice (apple pie spice), cocoa powder and ground almonds.

Using the beater attachment on your mixer, soften the butter, then add the sugar. Cream together. Slowly add the eggs, scraping down the bowl every so often to incorporate the ingredients fully. Fold in the whole almonds, the fruit mixture, lemon zest, 1 tbsp brandy and coffee essence.

Line a 20 x 6cm deep (8 x 2¼in) cake tin with parchment paper and spoon in the mixture. Bake on the middle shelf for at least 1 hour. Test the cake is cooked by inserting a small knife into the centre – it should come away clean. Allow the cake to cool in the tin before turning it out onto a wire rack. Strip off the parchment paper. Dot all over with a pastry brush dipped in a mixture of sugar syrup and 1 tbsp brandy, to help keep the cake moist.

Serves 10

30g (1oz) whole almonds
280g (10oz) currants
100g (3½oz) sultanas (golden raisins)
170g (6oz) raisins
70g (2½oz) mixed (candied) citrus peel
70g (2½oz) glacé (candied) cherries
170g (1½ cups) plain (all-purpose) flour, sifted
¼ tsp baking powder
¼ tsp table salt
1 tsp mixed spice (apple pie spice)
1½ tsp unsweetened cocoa powder
25g (1oz) ground almonds
160g (11 tbsp) unsalted butter
160g (generous ¾ cup) soft brown sugar
3 eggs, lightly beaten
grated zest of 1 large lemon
1 tbsp brandy
1 tsp coffee essence
sugar syrup (*see page 23*), made with 50g (¼ cup) caster (superfine) sugar and 50ml (3 tbsp + 1 tsp) water
1 tbsp brandy or similar spirit

CARROT & WALNUT CAKE

I like to use dark brown sugar to give extra depth to this classic recipe.

Preheat the oven to 170°C/340°F/Gas 3. Combine the eggs with the sugar and olive oil. Add the honey and vanilla essence.

Sift together the two lots of flour, baking powder and bicarbonate of soda (baking soda) and salt. Add the carrots, walnuts and sultanas (golden raisins), and mix well. Line an 18 x 7 x 8cm deep (7¼ x 2¾ x 3in) loaf tin with parchment paper. Pour in the mixture. Stir to ensure the walnuts are not all at the bottom. Bake on the middle shelf for approximately 40 minutes.

To test the cake is cooked, gently push a knife through to the centre – it should come away clean. Leave to cool in the tin for 20 minutes, then turn out onto a wire rack and strip off the parchment paper. If you wish, add a cream cheese topping (follow the recipe for the Peppermint Cream Cheese Topping on page 12 but leave out the peppermint essence and colouring).

Serves 8

2 eggs
155g (generous ¾ cup) dark brown sugar
145ml (½ cup + 1 tbsp) olive oil
1 generous tbsp honey
½ tsp vanilla essence
120g (¾ cup) wholemeal (whole-wheat) flour
40g (⅓ cup) plain (all-purpose) flour
½ tsp baking powder
½ tsp bicarbonate of soda (baking soda)
½ tsp table salt
125g (4½ oz) carrots, grated
50g (1¾ oz) walnuts, chopped
45g (1½ oz) sultanas (golden raisins)

BANANA LOAF

The perfect accompaniment to a cup of tea.

Preheat the oven to 170ºC/340ºF/Gas 3. Purée one banana. In a mixing bowl, cream the butter and sugar together until light and fluffy. Add the ground hazelnuts, followed by the eggs. Sift the flour, salt, bicarbonate of soda (baking soda) and baking powder into the mixture and mix together well. Mix in the sour cream, followed by the banana purée.

Line an 18 x 7 x 8cm deep (7$\frac{1}{4}$ x 2$\frac{3}{4}$ x 3in) loaf tin with parchment paper. Pour in the mixture. Slice the remaining banana and decorate the top. Bake on the middle shelf for 45 minutes to 1 hour. To test the loaf is cooked, gently push a knife through to the centre – it should come away clean. Leave to cool in the tin for 20 minutes, then turn out onto a wire rack and strip off the parchment paper.

Serves 8

2 bananas
150g (10 tbsp) unsalted butter
230g (generous 1 cup) caster (superfine) sugar
50g (1$\frac{3}{4}$oz) ground hazelnuts
2 eggs, lightly beaten
175g (1$\frac{1}{2}$ cups) plain (all-purpose) flour
1 tsp table salt
1 tsp bicarbonate of soda (baking soda)
1 tsp baking powder
135ml ($\frac{1}{2}$ cup + 1 tbsp) sour cream

LEMON DRIZZLE CAKE

I was taught to bake this gem of a cake in Paris more than 20 years ago. Delicately fragranced with lemon zest, it has won many hearts along the way. It's also become Marco Pierre White's favourite teatime treat.

Preheat the oven to 160°C/325°F/Gas 2½. In a mixing bowl, beat the eggs and slowly add the sugar, salt, flour and baking powder. Add the melted butter to the mixture, then pour in the cream and the lemon zest. Pour the mixture into a lightly greased 18 x 7 x 8cm deep (7¼ x 2¾ x 3in) loaf tin and bake on the middle shelf for about 45 minutes. To test the cake is cooked, gently push a knife through to the centre – it should come away clean. Leave to cool in the tin for 15 minutes, then turn out onto a wire rack.

While the cake is baking, make the lemon drizzle by boiling the water and the sugar together to 140°C/285°F, testing with a probe thermometer (*see page 8*), then add the lemon juice. Boil for about 10 minutes. Remove from the heat. Brush plenty of lemon drizzle onto the cake immediately after removing it from the oven. As well as putting a nice shine on the cake, the drizzle is absorbed into the cake, which helps to keep it moist.

Serves 8

3 eggs
230g (generous 1 cup) caster (superfine) sugar
pinch of table salt
180g (1½ cups) plain (all-purpose) flour, sifted
1 tsp baking powder
70g (6 tbsp) unsalted butter, melted
100ml (scant ½ cup) double (heavy) cream
grated zest of 2 lemons

For the lemon drizzle
100ml (scant ½ cup) water
75g (6 tbsp) caster (superfine) sugar
50ml (3 tbsp + 1 tsp) lemon juice

PARKIN

With its moist treacle (molasses) flavour, this is a must on a winter's day.

Preheat the oven to 170°C/340°F/Gas 3. Sift together the flour, spices, salt and bicarbonate of soda (baking soda), and then add the oatmeal (ground oats). In a pan, melt the butter, treacle (molasses) and sugar. Add the milk and stir in the dry ingredients, followed by the egg. Mix briskly together and pour into an 18 x 7 x 8cm deep (7¼ x 2¾ x 3in) loaf tin lined with parchment paper. Bake on the middle shelf for approximately 50 minutes.

To test the cake is cooked, gently push a knife through to the centre – it should come away clean. Leave to cool in the tin for 20 minutes, then turn out onto a wire rack and strip off the parchment paper.

Opposite: Lemon Drizzle Cake

Serves 10

225g (2 cups) plain (all-purpose) flour
1 tsp mixed spice (apple pie spice)
1 tsp ground cinnamon
1 tsp ground ginger
½ tsp table salt
1 tsp bicarbonate of soda (baking soda)
225g (8oz) oatmeal (ground oats)
150g (10 tbsp) unsalted butter
180g (½ cup) black treacle (molasses)
110g (generous ½ cup) soft brown sugar
150ml (⅔ cup) whole milk
1 egg, lightly beaten

BATTENBURG

Sometimes known as window cake, this is a traditional offering for afternoon tea that takes a little while to make but is well worth the effort.

Preheat the oven to 170°C/340°F/Gas 3. Cream the butter and sugar together until light and fluffy. Then beat in the eggs slowly and fold in the flour. Pour half of the mixture into a lightly greased loaf tin measuring 26 x 7 x 8cm deep (10¼ x 2¾ x 3in). Add a few drops of red food colouring to the remainder of the mixture until it is the desired shade of pink – I like quite a strong shade. Pour into a second lightly greased loaf tin of the same size.

Bake on the middle shelf for about 20–25 minutes. If they are ready, the sponges will spring back when pressed lightly. Leave in the tins for a couple of minutes before turning out onto a wire rack.

When cooled, using a serrated-edged knife, square off the sponges and cut both in half lengthways. Warm the jam, then paint the inside edges of the sponges with some of it – be careful not to use too much. Stick the sponges together to form the traditional chequerboard pattern.

Place the marzipan in a bowl. Add 2–3 drops of red food colouring and work it into the marzipan with your hands. Roll out a sheet of marzipan approximately 5mm (¼in) thick to cover the cake. Brush the top of the cake with more jam and turn the cake upside down onto the edge of the marzipan. Brush the remaining sides with the resto of the jam and carefully roll the cake in the marzipan. Cut neatly round the edges, smooth over gently with your hand and leave to set in the fridge for approximately 1 hour.

Serves 8

175g (¾ cup) unsalted butter
175g (generous ¾ cup) caster (superfine) sugar
3 eggs
175g (1½ cups) self-raising flour, sifted
red food colouring
100g (3½ oz) seedless apricot or raspberry jam
250g (9oz) pack ready-made marzipan (available from most supermarkets)

cookies, bars & bites

FLORENTINES

A crunchy cookie bursting with flavour, made with a classic Florentine mix.

Preheat the oven to 170°C/340°F/Gas 3. Spread the almonds, hazelnuts and pistachios on a baking tray and toast them on the middle shelf of the oven for 15 minutes or until golden brown.

In a pan, warm the butter and glucose together, then stir in the icing (confectioners') sugar, toasted nuts and mixed (candied) citrus peel. Leave to cool. Either arrange the mixture in balls and bake on a non-stick tray so that they spread out naturally as they cook, or place in small, individual non-stick moulds to give a little more depth and form.

Bake on the middle shelf for approximately 20 minutes. Turn out onto a wire rack and leave to cool. Either serve as they are or dip in melted dark or white chocolate. Alternatively, place the melted chocolate in a piping (pastry) bag and, with a small nozzle (tip), pipe your own decoration.

Makes 10

40g (1 1/4 oz) flaked (slivered) almonds
40g (1 1/4 oz) flaked (slivered) hazelnuts
40g (1 1/4 oz) pistachios, chopped
125g (2/3 cup) unsalted butter
2 tbsp liquid glucose
150g (1 1/4 cups) icing (confectioners') sugar, sifted
30g (1oz) mixed (candied) citrus peel
100g (3 1/2 oz) 70% cocoa dark (bittersweet) or white chocolate, melted (optional)

NUT BROWNIES

Great in lunch boxes or picnic hampers – few can resist them!

Preheat the oven to 160°C/325°F/Gas 2 1/2. Soften the butter in a bowl with a spatula, and add the sugar and melted chocolate. Slowly beat in the eggs and vanilla essence. Sift the flour and cocoa powder together and fold into the wet mixture. Add the nuts and pour into a lightly greased 24cm (9 1/2 in) square roasting tin. Bake on the middle shelf for 40 minutes.

To test it is cooked, gently push a knife through to the centre – it should come away clean. Turn out onto a wire rack and leave to cool. Cut into 14 squares.

Makes 14

340g (1 1/2 cups) unsalted butter, melted
680g (3 cups + 5 tbsp) caster (superfine) sugar
540g (1lb 3oz) 70% cocoa dark (bittersweet) chocolate, melted
6 eggs
1 tsp vanilla essence
150g (1 1/4 cups) plain (all-purpose) flour
150g (5 1/2 oz) unsweetened cocoa powder
100g (3 1/2 oz) whole hazelnuts, chopped
100g (3 1/2 oz) flaked (slivered) almonds

Opposite: Florentines; Nut Brownies illustrated on pages 52–3

TRADITIONAL SHORTBREAD

A melt-in-the-mouth traditional recipe that's deliciously crumbly.

Preheat the oven to 160°C/325°F/Gas 2½. In a mixing bowl, soften the butter with your hands, then add the sugar. Using a wooden spoon, cream together with the butter. Add the flour and semolina. With your fingers and thumbs, work the mixture until it resembles fine breadcrumbs. Bring together and work a little on a floured surface. Wrap in clingfilm (plastic wrap) and place in the fridge to rest for a good hour.

Roll the mixture into a circle to fit a 16cm (6½in) non-stick cake tin. Place in the tin and press with your fingers to the edges of the tin. Score the biscuit with a knife into eight wedges and score decorative marks with a fork. Bake on the middle shelf for about 20 minutes. (Ideally, shortbread should be pale, so as soon as colour starts to appear, remove from the oven.) Turn out onto a wire rack and leave to cool, but if the score marks have disappeared a little, go over them again now while the biscuit is still soft. Cut into eight wedges.

Serves 8

215g (1 cup) unsalted butter
100g (½ cup) caster (superfine) sugar
200g (1¾ cups) plain (all-purpose) flour
100g (3½ oz) semolina

MILLIONAIRE'S SHORTBREAD

Golden crunch, creamy caramel and sweet chocolate – perfection.

Preheat the oven to 170°C/340°F/Gas 3. For the base, cream the butter and sugar together in a mixing bowl until light and fluffy, then add the egg yolk and double cream. Stir in the flour. Using your fingers and thumbs, work the mixture until it resembles fine breadcrumbs. Bring together and work a little on a floured surface. Wrap in clingfilm (plastic wrap) and place in the fridge to rest.

To make the caramel, melt the butter in a pan, add the sugar, golden (light corn) syrup and condensed milk, and stir continuously on a low heat until it turns a caramel colour. Remove from the heat and leave the mixture in the pan. (It is worth testing a small amount to see if it will set in the fridge before removing completely from the heat.) This mixture can catch very easily, so take care – if you notice any small black dots, change your pan, as this means the mixture is catching, which will spoil the flavour.

Roll the shortbread mixture to 1cm (^{1}/$_2$in) thick and press down into a 24cm (9^1/$_2$in) square non-stick tin. Bake on the middle shelf until light brown. Leave to cool. Pour over the warm caramel, lightly shaking the tin to ensure an even covering. Leave to cool, then put in the fridge to set.

For the topping, melt the chocolate and butter in a mixing bowl over a bain-marie (water bath). Pour over the chilled caramel and shortbread. Place in the fridge until set, then slice into 16 bars.

Makes 16 bars

For the shortbread base
200g (scant 1 cup) unsalted butter
100g (^{1}/$_2$ cup) caster (superfine) sugar
1 egg yolk
1 tsp double (heavy) cream
225g (2 cups) plain (all-purpose) flour

For the caramel
180g (^{3}/$_4$ cup) unsalted butter
75g (6 tbsp) caster (superfine) sugar
50ml (3 tbsp) golden (light corn) syrup
350ml (scant 1^1/$_2$ cups) condensed milk

For the topping
250g (9oz) 60% cocoa dark (bittersweet) chocolate
50g (^{1}/$_4$ cup) unsalted butter

FRENCH MADELEINES

Madeleines are bite-sized, delicate sponges made in distinctive scallop shell moulds and best enjoyed fresh from the oven, when they're still lovely and warm. In France, they are often eaten dipped in coffee or tea.

Preheat the oven to 220°C/425°F/Gas 7. Make the beurre noisette (*see right*) and leave it to cool.

Meanwhile, whisk the eggs and sugar together in a mixing bowl. Add the flour, baking powder, milk and zests, followed by the cooled beurre noisette. Mix together.

Place the madeleine moulds in the freezer for about 10 minutes, then brush them quickly and thoroughly with melted butter. Return to the freezer for 5 minutes, remove and repeat the process, but this time follow with a good drenching of flour. Knock off the excess flour and return to the freezer for a few more minutes.

Using a medium piping nozzle (tip), pipe the mixture into the chilled moulds, being careful not to overfill. Bake on the middle shelf. When the madeleines are golden brown, remove and immediately knock out onto a wire rack.

Madeleines are delicious served hot – with your favourite topping; plain, with a little custard; sprinkled with icing (confectioners') sugar; or dipped in chocolate and reluctantly shared with the kids!

The secret to good madeleines is not only a hot oven but also well-buttered and floured moulds, so that the cakes can be removed easily after baking. Some people prefer to use non-stick madeleine moulds but I find that the non-stick layer eventually erodes. Never use a scourer to wash non-stick moulds – simply soak them and then sponge off any residue.

Makes 26

For the beurre noisette
125g (^{2}/$_3$ cup) unsalted butter

Place the butter in a pan and bring to the boil. Keep boiling until it turns a light brown. Remove from the heat. It's worth scraping down the sides of the pan thoroughly to include the residue from the boiling butter. Pour into a cold pan to prevent further cooking.

For the sponge
4 eggs
200g (1 cup) caster (superfine) sugar
250g (2^1/$_4$ cups) plain (all-purpose) flour, sifted
2 tsp baking powder
50ml (3 tbsp + 1 tsp) whole milk
grated zest of 1 orange
grated zest of 1 lemon

FINANCIERS

Traditional French sponge teacakes with a distinctive nutty taste from the beurre noisette. When dipped in a blend of dark rum and sugar syrup straight from the oven, these simple sponges become a luxurious delicacy.

Preheat the oven to 200°C/400°F/Gas 6. Using a mixer, beat the egg whites until they start to foam but are not whipped, then add the sugar and beat. Stop the mixer, scrape down the bowl, then beat again to ensure the ingredients are fully amalgamated. Gradually add the ground almonds and flour, beat rapidly for a short time until thoroughly mixed, then add the cooled beurre noisette.

Add the sultanas (golden raisins) to the sugar syrup and bring to the boil. Leave to cool. Drain and add to the mixture, making sure the sultanas are thoroughly incorporated. Spoon the mixture into 8 x 3 x 3cm deep (3 x 1$\frac{1}{4}$ x 1$\frac{1}{4}$in) silicone moulds (*see page* 8) – I find silicone ones easier to use and clean. Place the moulds on a baking tray and bake on the middle shelf for about 20 minutes. Remove from the oven and turn out onto a wire rack.

During my time at Le Gavroche restaurant, as soon as we had removed the financiers from the oven, we would dip them in an equal mixture of dark rum and sugar syrup – delicious. Alternatively, you can just brush them with apricot jam.

Makes 12

6 egg whites
150g ($\frac{3}{4}$ cup) caster (superfine) sugar
60g (2oz) ground almonds
60g (9 tbsp) plain (all-purpose) flour, sifted
beurre noisette (*see page 58*), made with
    150g (10 tbsp) unsalted butter, cooled
sugar syrup (*see page 23*), made with 100g
    (generous $\frac{1}{2}$ cup) caster (superfine)
    sugar and 100ml (6 tbsp + 2 tsp) water
150g (5$\frac{1}{2}$oz) sultanas (golden raisins)

ECCLES CAKES

The look of the currants gives these their nickname of 'squashed fly cakes'!

Preheat the oven to 180°C/350°F/Gas 4. Mix all the dry ingredients together, then add the melted butter.

Roll out the puff pastry to 3mm (⅛in) thick. Allow to rest for 30 minutes in the fridge. Cut out into 9cm (3½in) discs (there should be approximately 10). Place on a baking tray and leave to rest for a further 30 minutes in the fridge.

Using a tablespoon, spoon out the mixture and roll into balls. Place a pastry disc on a floured work surface and lightly egg-wash the edge. Press the ball of mixture into the centre and flatten with the heel of your hand. Fold the edges of the pastry around the mixture, covering all the mixture. Press down again, turn over and then press again. Repeat for the remaining discs. Place the cakes on a non-stick tray, brush with milk and sprinkle with a little caster (superfine) sugar. Bake on the middle shelf for 20 minutes until nice and golden. Turn out onto a wire rack.

Makes 10

140g (¾ cup) soft light brown sugar
1 tsp cinnamon
½ tsp mixed spice (apple pie spice)
140g (5oz) currants
85g (3oz) mixed (candied) citrus peel
85g (7 tbsp) unsalted butter, melted
500g (1lb 2oz) pack puff pastry
1 egg, lightly beaten
a little milk
caster (superfine) sugar, for sprinkling

ACKNOWLEDGMENTS

Firstly, thanks to my publisher, Jacqui Small, for believing in me and giving me this wonderful opportunity. Also, thanks to her team: Jo Copestick, Judith Hannam and Helen Ridge for their enduring patience, and also Ashley Western for his vision and humour. Thanks, too, to Sian Irvine for her fantastic photography.

To Marco Pierre White – I will be always grateful for the opportunities he has given me over the years, the friendship he has shown me and the passion he has inspired in me to cook great food.

To my suppliers Rod and Des at Hansens Kitchen Equipment, Dave at Cream of the Crop, and Pat at Ritters – thank you for the constant humour and the quality goods.

I must also thank the boys who have helped me with this book for their commitment and support on shoot days: Matt Brown, Simon Cotterill and Arran Greig.

Special thanks and love to my wife, Penny, whose tenacity and drive have made this book possible, and to my two munchkins, Alfie and Nell, my best critics.

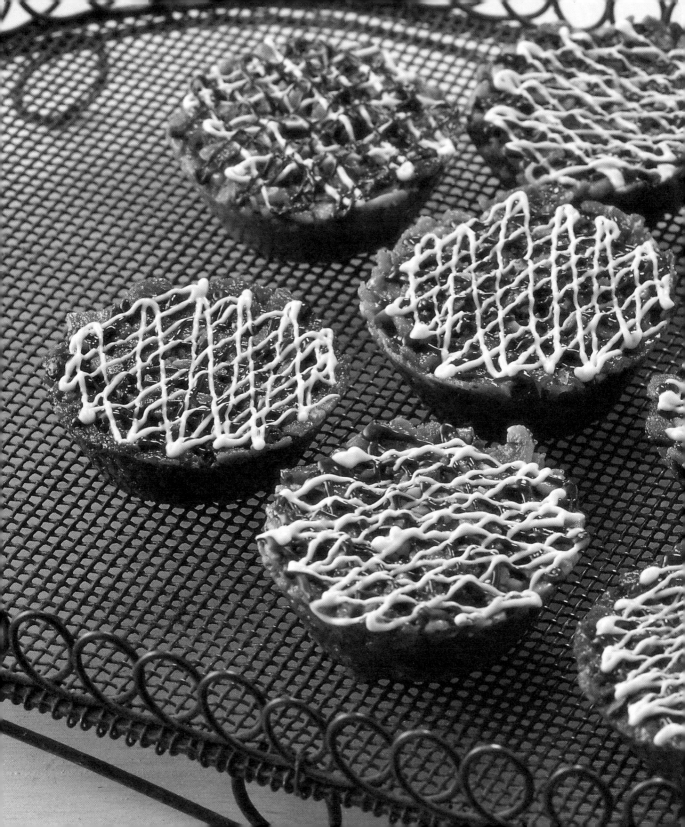